21st
Century
Skills Library

ANIMAL INVADERS

AFRICANIZED HONEY BEE

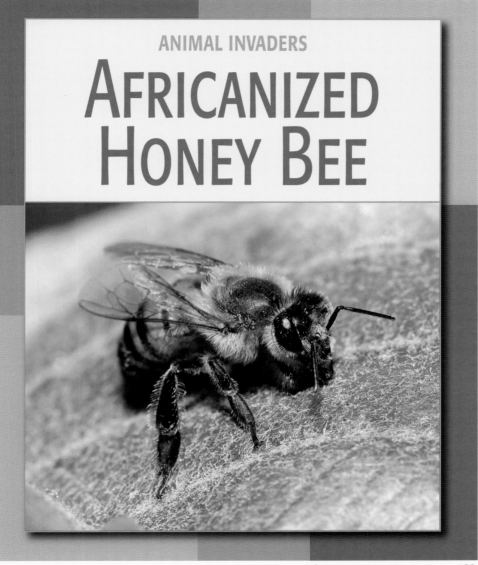

Barbara A. Somervill

Cherry Lake Publishing
Ann Arbor, Michigan

Published in the United States of America by Cherry Lake Publishing
Ann Arbor, MI
www.cherrylakepublishing.com

Content Adviser: Eric C. Mussen, Extension Apiculturist, Department of Entomology, University of California, Davis, California

Please note: Our map is as up-to-date as possible at the time of publication.

Photo Credits: Cover and pages 1 and 26, © iStockphoto.com/jamesbenet; pages 4, 12, and 16, © Rodney Mehring, used under license from Shutterstock, Inc.; page 6, © iStockphoto.com/varela; pages 8, 10, 14, and 18, © Scott Bauer, USDA Agricultural Research Service, Bugwood.org; page 20, © iStockphoto.com/Westhoff; pages 22 and 25, © Division of Plant Industry Archive, Florida Department of Agriculture and Consumer Services, Bugwood.org

Map by XNR Productions Inc.

Library of Congress Cataloging-in-Publication Data
Somervill, Barbara A.
 Africanized Honey Bee / by Barbara A. Somervill.
  p. cm.—(Animal invaders)
 Includes index.
 ISBN-13: 978-1-60279-117-6
 ISBN-10: 1-60279-117-1
 1. Africanized honeybee—Juvenile literature. I. Title. II. Series.
 QL568.A6S764 2008
 595.79'9—dc22   2007034573

*Cherry Lake Publishing would like to acknowledge the work of
The Partnership for 21st Century Skills.
Please visit www.21stcenturyskills.org for more information.*

TABLE OF CONTENTS

CHAPTER ONE

BEES, BEES, BEES!

An Africanized honey bee hive hangs from a tree.

In Copperas Cove, Texas, a couple is recovering from stings from hundreds of bees. Doctors stopped counting stings on the woman after they reached 500. Her husband has more than 100 stings—on each arm. Both had bees in their mouths and all over their faces. They were just getting into their car when they got the first stings. Nearby was a hollow tree that served as the bees' nest.

The bees were Africanized honey bees. These bees are an invasive species. An invasive species is any plant or animal that moves into—and takes over—an area where it does not naturally live.

In the town of San Ignacio, Mexico, a local beekeeper offers cash rewards for anyone who destroys wild bees' nests. The beekeeper fears what might happen if the Africanized bees take over his hives. In all, 650 wild nests are found.

Another beekeeper in Mexico rents his hives out to farmers for pollinating their crops. His hives have already

It takes an expert to remove an established nest and its bees. This is not a job for a can of insect spray from the supermarket. Pest controllers must wear extra-heavy clothing, gloves, and a screened head covering. They may first carefully "smoke" the hive because smoke calms the bees. Once the bees have been removed, the pest controller gets rid of all traces of the nest and seals off the space. Why do you think it's important to seal off the space?

All beekeepers wear some protective gear. When dealing with Africanized hives, beekeepers protect their entire bodies.

been "Africanized" by invading bees. That means the

Africanized bees have bred with his pure European honey

bees. The resulting bees do an excellent job of pollinating

crops. But they are much more easily threatened, or **defensive**, than pure European bees.

Tonight, this beekeeper will move his hives to a cucumber field. He puts on his protective gear. Beekeepers who deal with Africanized bees must be very careful. They move the hives in the dark when the bees are home for the night and less active. This invading species brings many changes to the world it takes over.

Learning & Innovation Skills

Africanized honey bees prick their victims with stingers. The stinger has barbs that hold it in the victim's skin. Pouches or sacs of venom are attached to the stingers. Once the bee pulls away, a muscle remains, pumping the poison through the stinger. What are some other animals that defend themselves with poison? What else do these animals have in common?

CHAPTER TWO

THE WORLD OF AFRICANIZED BEES

An Africanized honey bee (left) and a European honey bee stand on honeycomb. Despite color differences between these two bees, it is usually not possible to tell them apart with the naked eye.

North and South America have only one species of honey bee. But there are a number of mixed-breed bees, including the Africanized honey bee—*Apis mellifera scutellata*. Africanized bees can mate with and produce young with all common honey bees.

Africanized bees are about 0.75 inch (2 centimeters) long. They have a brownish, fuzzy appearance. Unfortunately, the only way to tell an Africanized bee from a European bee is under a microscope.

Honey bees go through four stages of life. A honey bee starts as an egg. It hatches as a wormlike larva and needs time to grow. Then the larva changes into a pupa. After a time, it finally emerges as an adult.

Bees live in colonies. A colony usually has 10,000 to 50,000 bees. Each colony has only one queen. Colonies also have male drones and worker bees. Worker bees are females that are unable to produce young.

Most eggs in a colony become worker bees. A few will become drones, which are needed to mate with the queen. Others are fed special food to become queen larvae. It takes fewer than 19 days to change from egg to adult worker bee. It takes 15 days for a queen to mature.

Africanized honey bees surround a European honey bee queen (identified with a pink dot). In the United States, Africanized honey bees have mated with European honey bees and spread.

Worker bees are constantly replaced as they die. Drones, which are only produced when needed for mating, live 35 days. Queen honey bees live one or more years. The queen's long life span helps the colony survive.

When a queen dies, new possible queens emerge. The first two queens that reach the adult stage battle to the death. The one that survives becomes queen. For the rest of her life, she may produce as many as 1,500 eggs a day.

When a colony becomes too large, part of the colony, along with the old queen, breaks away in a swarm. The bees are preparing to find a new place to live. They send scout bees to search for a new nesting site.

Scientists do not fully understand how Africanized bees make colonies. The Africanized bees may swarm as often as six times a year. European honey bees rarely swarm more than once. Africanized bees build nests in any convenient crook or cranny. They nest in barns, trees, cracks of buildings, drainage pipes, flowerpots, and birdhouses and

Bees produce honey as well as beeswax for things such as cosmetics, candles, and wood polish. As pollinators, they affect the quantity and quality of fruit, vegetables, and nut crops. What other animals produce things that humans use? What other animals help in pollination?

Africanized honey bees are not picky about nesting sites. Here, they built a nest in a space between rocks.

under mobile homes. European honey bees are much choosier about their nest sites.

As soon as an Africanized bee swarm finds a new location, it starts building a new nest. The bees are less likely to sting in this early stage. They will be more defensive later, when the colony is up and going and they have eggs. But it can be easy to provoke even newly arrived bees to protect their nest.

Several things make Africanized bees much more dangerous than ordinary honey bees. Just about any vibration, unfamiliar smell, or movement near the hive sets off the bees. They defend in larger groups. They are considered 10 times as likely to sting as European honey bees. Africanized bees have been known to chase a victim as far as 1,320 feet (400 meters) from the hive!

Like other bees, Africanized bees can sting only once. Through their stingers, they inject the same venom that other honey bees do. When any honey bee stings a victim, it releases a chemical called a pheromone that riles up other bees. The danger from Africanized bees is not a single sting but the combined venom of many stings.

After stinging, a bee leaves a stinger behind. The bee then bleeds to death. A new worker bee quickly replaces it.

CHAPTER THREE

Bee Invaders

A researcher works with European honey bees as part of a U.S. project to learn more about Africanized honey bees.

Africanized bees do not come from Africa, although their distant relatives did. In 1956, scientists brought African honey bees to São Paulo, Brazil. They hoped to mate these African honey bees with local honey bees to create a mixed-breed bee that produced more wax and more honey. They also wanted a bee that would do well in Brazil's hot, humid weather.

A year later, the scientists had produced bees that were hardier but not as productive as they had hoped. The mixed-breed bees, called Africanized bees, were held in quarantine up to this point. Then some of the bees escaped. They quickly bred with Brazilian honey bees—and became a threatening invasive species.

The bees multiplied quickly in the warm Brazilian climate. They found plenty of food throughout the year. Within a year, they had increased their range by nearly 300 miles (480 kilometers) in nearly a full circle. In Buenos Aires, Argentina, the Africanized bees stopped their progress. Scientists thought that the weather might have been too cold for the bees to advance farther south.

To the west and north, no such barriers existed. Africanized bees advanced from almost 100 miles (161 km) to nearly 300 miles (480 km) every year. Bad weather may have slowed down the bees, but it did not stop them.

Africanized honey bees have spread north from South America, where they were first introduced.

Each time the Africanized bees met honey bees, they invaded the nests and created a variety of Africanized bee.

By the mid-1980s, Africanized honey bees had expanded their range deep into Mexico. A mild climate and a year-round growing cycle in some areas of Mexico appealed to the bees. By 1990, the bees had reached Sinaloa, a region of western Mexico with lots of fruit and vegetable crops. From 1988 to 1995, more than 150 Mexicans suffered serious attacks from Africanized bees.

The Africanized honey bees were first reported in the United States in Hidalgo, Texas, in 1990. The bees moved into New Mexico, Arizona, and California. Rivers, deserts, and high mountain ranges did not stop their advance.

By 2004, the bees had invaded Nevada, Oklahoma, and Alabama. A year later, they were in Florida, Louisiana, and Arkansas. Scientists expect the bees to spread through the southern half of the United States. How quickly that will happen is a difficult question to answer.

Life & Career Skills

For several years before Africanized bees arrived in the United States, Mexican beekeepers were dealing with this challenge. They had to build on what they already knew about bees to learn how to handle Africanized bees. They came up with a process called requeening. That's when a colony's Africanized queen is replaced with a European queen. The hope is that requeening produces more peaceful bees. So far, the beekeepers have had great success.

CHAPTER FOUR

MAJOR PROBLEMS

Scientists working for the U.S. Agricultural Research Service use smoke and a special vacuum to collect Africanized honey bees for further study.

Scientists have monitored, mapped, and studied no insect as closely as the Africanized honey bee in the past 15 years. There are many reasons for this interest. Africanized bees injure—and sometimes kill—humans, livestock, and pets. They also change the way beekeeping is done wherever they invade, and they threaten farming practices.

This small bee has appeared in countless news stories, on thousands of Web sites, and in low-budget horror movies. People call them killer bees. But in fact, despite hundreds of serious stinging attacks, only 18 deaths have been connected to Africanized honey bee stings since 1990. (An American is more likely to be struck by lightning than killed by Africanized bees.) A healthy adult would need to receive more than 300 stings to be killed. Some people have survived more than 1,000 stings! However, Africanized bees do cause major problems.

The biggest problem is that they upset the way beekeepers and farmers do

21st Century Content

What to do if you see a swarm of honey bees heading your way:

- Run to shelter, such as a car or building.
- Do not go underwater. The bees may wait for you to surface for air.
- Cover your face to prevent stinging on the eyes, nose, or mouth or in the throat.
- Do not wave your arms. Movement attracts the bees.
- Go to the hospital immediately if you have several stings.

Farmers in Michigan have set out hives full of bees to pollinate the blossoms in a cherry orchard.

business. Bee colonies are usually rented out to farmers, orchard owners, and citrus growers during their most important pollination periods. In California alone, there are 1.4 million hive rentals a year. Without honey bees to pollinate fruit, vegetable, and nut crops, there would be fewer farm products and of worse quality.

Sometimes colonies leave their hives altogether. The Africanized bees are more sensitive to disturbances than

European honey bees. An Africanized bee colony may depart if there are vibrations, pests, fire, or damage to the nest structure. Then beekeepers must restock the empty hive by splitting a current colony into two. It takes a long time to rebuild a lost colony, which means a loss of income for the beekeeper.

While Mexican beekeepers and farmers have adjusted well to the arrival of Africanized bees, beekeepers and farmers in California are facing a more severe situation. California agriculture needs 50 times the number of rental bees for pollination as Mexico. Beekeepers in California are having a hard time meeting the state's need.

Learning & Innovation Skills

Beekeepers and pest controllers are not the only ones who need to figure out ways to deal with Africanized bees. Firefighters, emergency medical teams, doctors, and nurses in areas where bee attacks have occurred are looking for better ways to protect residents and treat those who are stung. Can you think of some ways these professionals can prepare for Africanized bee attacks?

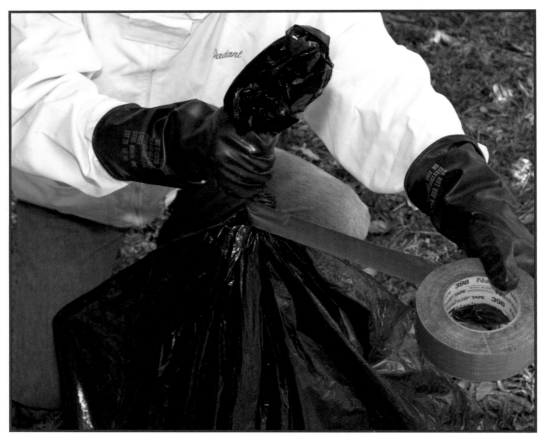

The collection and disposal of Africanized honey bees is very dangerous work best left to trained experts.

If California does not have enough hives to pollinate fruit, vegetable, and nut crops, what will happen to the state's agricultural economy? This is no small problem. Bees in California pollinate billions of dollars of crops.

Those crops include oranges, limes, lemons, avocados, almonds, cucumbers, squash, zucchini, plums, pears, peaches, and apples.

Africanized bees affect other fields, too. Firefighters, construction workers, and road builders have to be aware of the danger from bees at their workplaces. Africanized bees nest in holes in trees or the ground, in construction equipment, and in drainpipes under the road. While working, they might end up disturbing a bee colony. So they have learned what to do in case that happens.

Most deaths and serious stinging events have happened to ordinary citizens. Children, older people, and

those allergic to bee stings are at the greatest risk. The amount of venom from 10 stings has a greater effect on a 44-pound (20 kilogram) child than on a 132-pound (60 kg) adult. Older people have trouble getting away from the bees before being stung repeatedly. It is the number of stings that hurts these people. As for those allergic to honey bee stings, a single sting from any honey bee could be deadly.

In Tucson, Arizona, pest controllers had to remove a supersized nest of Africanized bees from a senior citizens' home. In western Texas, a man found a swarm in an empty mobile home on his property. The bees stung him badly after he tried to burn them out. Someone in Cooper City, Florida, found a large nest in a tree near a day care center. These are only a few of the Africanized bee stories. For people who live in the same areas as these bees, safety comes only from caution. Beware of bees!

CHAPTER FIVE

No Easy Answers

Traps for Africanized honey bee have had some success. Captured swarms are easily removed or destroyed with soapy water.

There are simply no easy answers to the Africanized bee problem. The bees cannot be poisoned, because that same poison would also kill European honey bees. And humans cannot feed themselves without honey bees. The salad on the dinner table, the vegetable on the side, and the apple pie for dessert all depend on the activity of honey bees.

Introducing species to new areas presents many challenges. The Africanized honey bee is only one of many animal invaders.

It is also impossible to stop the Africanized honey bees from spreading into more territory. No net, filter, or wall can stop a bee flying to a new location. Neither the California deserts nor the Mississippi River has stopped the bees from moving forward. So far, the only thing that seems to stop the advance of Africanized bees is a cold climate.

State and federal government agencies are monitoring the movements of Africanized bees. They cannot stop them, but they can warn people about Africanized bees moving into their areas. Then it is up to people to protect themselves.

So, stop, look, and listen. Before going into a wilderness area, park, or nearby ball field, check out the area. If bees are flying and buzzing in a group, do not enter the area. Check around your home to make sure bees have not begun building a nest in walls, trees, sheds, or barns. Never try to remove a bees' nest alone. Call in an expert.

Unfortunately, these animal invaders are here to stay. It's up to humans to solve the problems caused by introducing species where they don't belong.

In 1962, biologist Rachel Carson first published her book *Silent Spring* (Boston: Houghton Mifflin, 2002). The book told of a time in the future when there were no birds, or bees, or crops because of pesticides. Her vision began the environmental movement in the United States. She also wrote of the important role of bees: "The apple trees were coming into bloom but no bees droned among the blossoms, so there was no pollination and there would be no fruit." What do other animals do to help their ecosystem?

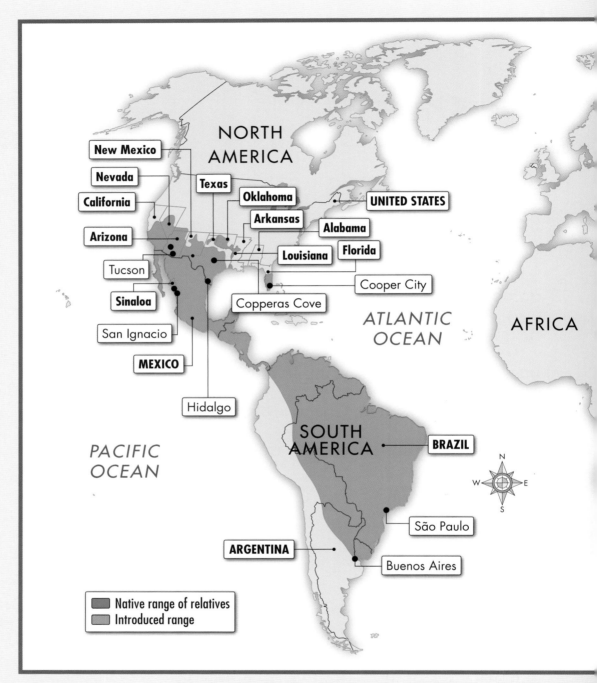

NORTH
AMERICA

New Mexico

Nevada

California

Texas

Oklahoma

UNITED STATES

Arizona

Arkansas

Alabama

Tucson

Louisiana

Florida

Sinaloa

Copperas Cove

Cooper City

San Ignacio

ATLANTIC
OCEAN

AFRICA

MEXICO

Hidalgo

PACIFIC
OCEAN

SOUTH
AMERICA

BRAZIL

N

W   E

S

São Paulo

ARGENTINA

Buenos Aires

■ Native range of relatives
■ Introduced range

This map shows where in the world the Africanized honey bee

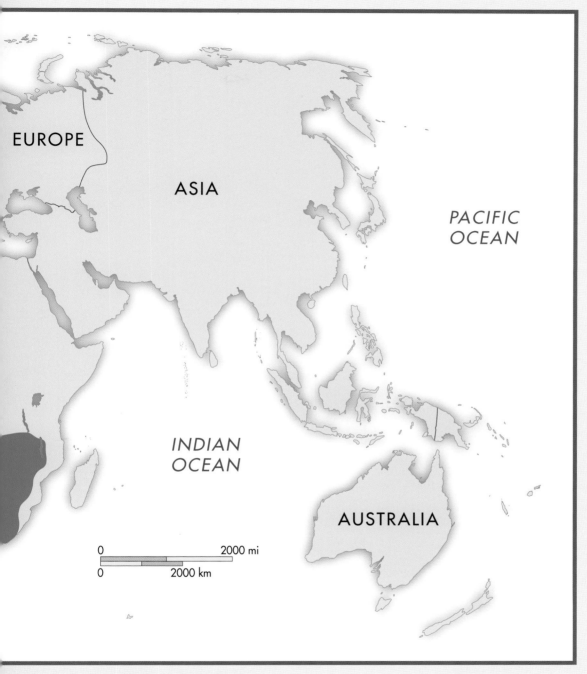

EUROPE

ASIA

PACIFIC
OCEAN

INDIAN
OCEAN

AUSTRALIA

0   2000 mi

0   2000 km

lives naturally and where it has invaded.

GLOSSARY

colonies (KOL-uh-neez) large groups of bees or other insects that live together

defensive (di-FEN-siv) committed to resisting or preventing an attack

drones (DROHNZ) male bees, especially honey bees, that can mate with the queen

ecosystem (EE-koh-siss-tuhm) a community of plants, animals, and other organisms together with their environment, working as a unit

larva (LAR-vuh) the newly hatched, wormlike form of many insects

mixed-breed (MIKST-BREED) having parents of different species or subspecies

pesticides (PESS-tuh-sides) chemical substances designed to kill pests, such as rats, mice, or insects

pheromone (FAIR-uh-moan) a chemical that is produced and given off by an animal to influence the behavior of others of the same species

pollinating (POL-uh-nay-ting) transferring pollen (a colored powder) from the male structure of a plant to the female structure for fertilization

pupa (PYOO-puh) the stage between larva and adult for some insects

quarantine (KWOR-uhn-teen) the prevention or tight control of the movement of people, plants, or animals to prevent spreading pests or a disease

queen (KWEEN) a female bee, wasp, or ant that can lay eggs in a colony

species (SPEE-sheez) a group of similar plants or animals

swarm (SWORM) a group of bees that leaves the nest and flies around, usually to find a new home

venom (VEN-uhm) poison produced by some snakes, bees, toads, and other animals

FOR MORE INFORMATION

Books

Allman, Toney. *Animals Attack: Killer Bees*. San Diego: KidHaven Press, 2004.

Landau, Elaine. *Killer Bees*. Berkeley Heights, NJ: Enslow Publishers, 2003.

Markle, Sandra. *Outside and Inside Killer Bees*. New York: Walker & Company, 2004.

Nichols, Catherine, ed. *Animal Planet: The Most Extreme Bugs*. San Francisco: Jossey-Bass, 2007.

Web Sites

Insecta Inspecta World: Africanized, Sometimes Called "Killer Bees"
www.insecta-inspecta.com/bees/killer/index.html
For answers to common questions about the Africanized bee

Texas A&M University Department of Entomology: Africanized Honey Bee
honeybee.tamu.edu/africanized/index.html
To learn about how to "bee-proof" your house and what to do if you get stung

USDA National Agricultural Library: Invasive Species—Africanized Honeybee
www.invasivespeciesinfo.gov/animals/afrhonbee.shtml
For the latest information and research about these bees,
maps, and frequently asked questions

INDEX

ABOUT THE AUTHOR

Barbara A. Somervill writes children's nonfiction books on a variety of topics. She is particularly interested in nature and foreign countries. Somervill believes that researching new and different topics makes writing every book an adventure. When she is not writing, Somervill is an avid reader and plays bridge.